CW01614566

Hallelujah

JOURNEYING THROUGH ADVENT
WITH HANDEL'S MESSIAH

DAVE & SALLY GOBBETT

10 Publishing
a division of 10 of those.com

To Ella-Beth, Owen, Barney & Noah.

'He tends his flock like a shepherd: he gathers the lambs in his arms and carries them close to his heart; he gently leads those that have young' (Isaiah 40:11, NIV).

We love you and pray you would experience this verse to be true, just as we have.

First published in Great Britain in 2025

British Library Cataloguing in Publication Data
A record for this book is available from the British Library

ISBN: 978-1-83728-086-5

Designed by Pete Barnsley (CreativeHoot.com)
Printed in Denmark

10Publishing, a division of 10ofthose.com
6b Upper Water Street, Newry, Co Down, Northern Ireland, BT34 1DJ
info@10ofthose.com | www.10ofthose.com

1 3 5 7 10 8 6 4 2

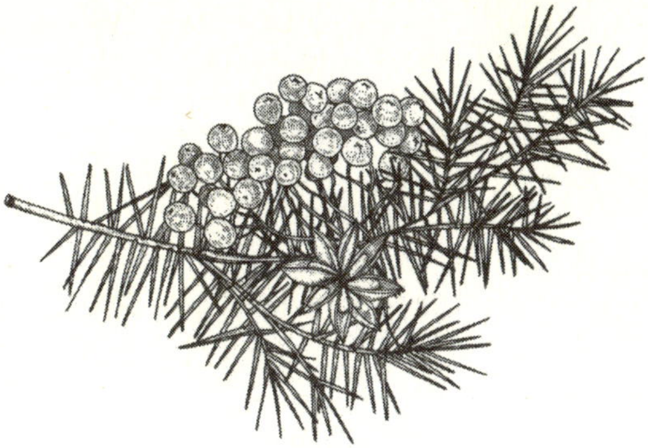

Preface

We have had a long and happy relationship with Handel's *Messiah*. Dave's parents used to play cassette tapes of it to send him to sleep as a child. It is the only piece of classical music he's ever bought on CD. And he writes his Sunday sermons most weeks with the *Messiah* playing in the background – so we're never surprised when George Frideric Handel ends up high on our Spotify most-played list each year. Sally has performed *Messiah* on a number of occasions, both as a soprano soloist and a chorus member. And we're pleased to say that the kids are beginning to catch the bug too!

Maybe you're already a convert, in which case you'll understand why Handel's *Messiah* is undoubtedly one of the most celebrated and beloved pieces of classical music in the English language. Handel composed the music for the oratorio in a marathon twenty-four-day writing stint in 1741, barely leaving his study. Maybe you still need convincing. If the *Messiah* is new to you, or perhaps you wouldn't call yourself a classical music fan, then please stay with us. We very much hope to bring this magnificent music, and its marvellous message, to a wider audience.

Every Christmas (and Easter), millions of people around the world – both believers and unbelievers – treat themselves to performances of the *Messiah*. One glorious movement follows another: the evocative 'Comfort Ye My People'; the rousing 'For unto Us a Child Is Born'; the exultant 'Rejoice Greatly, O Daughter of Zion'; the urgent 'All We Like Sheep Have Gone Astray'; the poignant 'He Trusted in God'; the victorious 'I know that My Redeemer Liveth'; not to mention the anthemic 'Hallelujah' chorus.

The genius and uniqueness of Handel's *Messiah* is that every single word is taken directly from the Bible. We have Handel's friend Charles Jennens to thank for that. He was the librettist. That is, he compiled the lyrics from the King James Version, two thirds of which come from the Old Testament. Together, Handel and Jennens have provided us with one of the earliest, and certainly most memorable, 'Bible overviews'. We'll trace through the theme of Messiah in three parts, which we're calling the Promise of the Messiah, the Passion of the Messiah and the People of the Messiah.

While the *Messiah* gives us rich biblical content, rarely do we take the opportunity to slow down and reflect on the meaning of each excerpt, mirrored in Handel's composition. This book is therefore made up of twenty-five devotions to be read during

Advent, plus a bonus introductory prelude for 30 November to whet your appetite, journeying through Handel's masterpiece. (There are actually over fifty movements in *Messiah*, so we've had to group some together and omit a few.) Each devotion includes the original biblical text Handel used, a brief meditation and a link to the music so you can listen along at home. Most days have between three and four minutes of music to listen to, though occasionally there are nearer ten minutes (and 'He Was Despised' is over eleven minutes on its own). While we pray that you'll benefit from simply reading the reflections, we believe that you'll get more from this devotion if you make the time to listen prayerfully to the pieces as well. We're convinced the fusion of music and meditation is extremely compelling. There is a QR code to the album we have used in preparing this book at the bottom of the Preface, performed by choral ensemble The Sixteen, which is available on Apple Music and Spotify.

If you'd like to think further about the history behind *Messiah*, we recommend looking at Charles King's *Every Valley: The Story of Handel's Messiah*. For a more in-depth look at the musicianship of the *Messiah* from a theological perspective, Lee Gatiss' beautifully presented edited work, *A Month with the Messiah: Reflections on Handel's Masterpiece*, is an excellent resource. It too has been designed to be used during Advent.

We would like to thank the many people who've made this short devotional possible: our loving parents, Geoff & Christine Gobbett and Nigel & Liz Jones, for exposing us to great music and great theology for as long as we can remember; our children, Ella-Beth, Owen, Barney & Noah for bearing with us and cheering us along the way; our friends at 10ofThose for bringing a vision to reality; our brothers and sisters at Highfields Church for sharing our journey with our Messiah all year round; ministry friends, Elspeth Pitt, Andrew Sach and Garry Williams for clarifying a few points of theology; and others who've prayed for us along the way. We thank God for giving gifts to mankind in the creative genius of Charles Jennens and George Frideric Handel, and for the voices and music with which to praise him. Above all, we thank God for our crucified, risen, reigning and returning Lord Jesus, whose saving and sustaining grace we seek to proclaim. 'Not to us, O Lord, not to us, but to your name be the glory, because of your love and faithfulness' (Psalm 115:1).

As we journey together through Handel's *Messiah* this Advent, over the same length of time that it took Handel to write the whole piece, it's our hope and prayer that you'd be struck afresh by the Messiah himself, as we await his coming again. May we all find ourselves caught up in that chorus of celebration and hope that lasts forever: hallelujah!

Cardiff
Easter 2025

30 November: Introduction

Overture [3:09]

'Are we nearly there yet?' Our extended families live at opposite ends of the country. Christmas holidays always involve the twelve-hour round trip between Cardiff and Newcastle. One infamous year in the Gobbett family saw Dave preaching on Christmas Day morning before a six-hour drive to the north-east, with one of our sons longingly cradling his unopened box of technic Lego for the whole journey. Long car journeys are wonderful training grounds for teaching you how to wait!

Advent is a time of waiting. The word literally means, 'coming'. As we wait the few short weeks for 25 December to arrive, and the children ask, 'How many more sleeps till Christmas?' we remember the long-awaited first coming of the Messiah. And we anticipate his long-awaited second coming. That first Christmas, believers had to wait hundreds of years for the birth of Jesus. We're already in the thousands as we look to his return.

There are over three minutes of wordless music before the first lyrics are sung in *Messiah*. This wait is purposeful, and Handel's musical choices are significant. Music has the power to touch the emotions, and Handel knew this. Mozart apparently said of him, 'Handel understands effect better than any of us – when he chooses, he strikes like a thunderbolt.' The musical style used here ('French Overture') was a typical two-part opening for Baroque stage music, popular in early-seventeenth-to-mid-eighteenth-century Europe. The first part features slow dotted rhythms (daaah da-daaah da-daaah da-daaah), characteristic of a sombre royal procession. The second part is an energetic fugue in which a short musical phrase is taken up and interwoven by successive instruments (listen out for more fugues as *Messiah* unfolds). Handel is setting the stage for a drama – the arrival of a king. But hanging over the upbeat fugue, a minor key leaves the listener with a sense of foreboding.

For what or whom are you waiting in this Advent season? The music of Handel's first movement charges us with this serious question. Are you waiting for the grandchildren to arrive? Are you counting down the days till the end of the school term? Are you simply looking forward to the food, the time off work, the presents? Or are you longing to relive, with expectant Israel, the arrival of her King and Saviour? Are you seeking to have your emotions grasped afresh by the narrative of the suffering, yet triumphant, Servant? Are you serious about preparing your heart and those of the people around you for his glorious second advent?

For some of us, it's easy to forget our returning King. We live as if the overture were an end in itself. We get comfortable or consumed in the here and now – whether we're over the moon at possibilities or overwhelmed by pressures. For others, the King can't return soon enough. We experience brokenness in the world, heaviness in our hearts and darkness all around. And we desperately pray, 'Come Lord Jesus'. The wait is lonely, confusing and painful. Whichever camp you find yourself in this Advent, let's pray that we would lift our eyes and ears to the Messiah whose arrival and passion will change the world forever.

PART 1

THE *Promise* OF THE *Messiah*

1 December

Tenor Solo [3:11] – Isaiah 40:1–3

> *Comfort ye, comfort ye my people, saith your God. Speak ye comfortably to Jerusalem, and cry unto her, that her warfare is accomplished, that her iniquity is pardoned. The voice of him that crieth in the wilderness; prepare ye the way of the Lord; make straight in the desert a highway for our God.*

The very first words that break the silence come from a lonely tenor. 'Comfort ye, comfort ye my people, saith your God,' he sings. Taken from Isaiah chapter 40, like several of the early pieces in *Messiah*, they parachute us into eighth-century BC turmoil. After years of spiritual compromise and divine warning, God's people have been trafficked into exile over five hundred miles away from home. For these refugees in Babylon, Solomon's temple is a distant memory. As are the sacrifices that took place there. As is the forgiveness that they secured. In their place it's all warfare (the KJV's way of referring to Israel's national strife) and iniquity (referring to their spiritual bankruptcy).

No doubt internal voices of guilt and shame would have crowded in. Feelings of regret and loss, confusion and fear. Why have we brought this on ourselves? Is it the end of the road spiritually? Can anything be done about our plight? Has God forgotten us? Is there any way home to a land of spiritual vitality again? Of course, we live in a very different time and place, but some of these questions may have a contemporary ring about them – perhaps even a personal one.

For those with ears to hear, the promise of comfort is given, three times over. The tenor voice triple underlines that God has not forgotten his people. Their long and wearying era of strife and sin is finally over, soon to be firmly in the rearview mirror. And rather than forever rubbing their noses in the past, God is ready and willing to move on. To the future we go! This is comfort indeed.

As you look back on the last year, maybe you too have felt somewhat distant from God, if you're honest. Happier times of closeness to God and spiritual vitality seem a distant memory. Perhaps it's because of choices you've made, or the choices of those around you. Perhaps it's just the weariness of trying to live for God when everything around you urges the opposite.

But God doesn't want us languishing in spiritual exile. He loves his people too much to leave them struggling alone. Which is why, if you listen closely, you'll hear a 'voice … that crieth in the wilderness; prepare ye the way of the Lord'. These words famously belong to John the Baptist and assure us that whoever we are, whatever we've done and however hard life has become, this Christmas our Lord is near. With the Messiah, help is never far away.

2 *December*

Tenor Aria [3:33] – Isaiah 40:4

> *Every valley shall be exalted, and every mountain and hill made low; the crooked straight, and the rough places plain.*

Several years ago, Barack Obama visited Cardiff. He stayed at Celtic Manor, the luxury hotel resort just outside Newport, which was the host venue for a NATO summit of world leaders. Years went into the planning. No expense was spared. The M4 motorway between Newport and Cardiff was temporarily reconfigured. The roads into Cardiff city centre had never looked better. There was not a pothole or roadwork in sight! Truly the rough places were made plain.

It's what happens when someone important is on the way. In today's meditation, Isaiah pictures creation getting ready for the arrival of the Lord. No expense is spared. Tectonic plates realign. Flawless tarmac rolls out as far as the eye can see. Nothing can delay or deter a God who is set on saving.

Maybe God feels far away right now. All you see are the hills and valleys in front of you, some of them as high as Mount Everest or as deep as the Grand Canyon. Hills of difficulty, valleys of despair. If there is a road between you and divine help, it feels crooked and rough and altogether treacherous and impassable. Can God really get past all the twisting and turning, the bumps and boulders, to reach us in our time of need?

He most certainly can. 'The LORD is near to all who call on him, to all who call on him in truth' writes the psalmist

(Psalm 145:18, NIV). Any distance between us and God is our problem, not his. If God wants to get through to us, no puny mountain or gaping ravine will slow him down.

That means no regrets we may have about yesterday will hold him back. No burdens of today will throw him off. No anxiety about tomorrow will overwhelm him. If creation itself can be moulded like putty to clear the way for God to get through, then you can be certain divine aid is close at hand.

Handel captures such divine bulldozing brilliantly, with the tenor's aria recreating the Scripture musically. Why not listen again and observe that the melody goes up for the word 'exalted', down for the words 'made low', meanders up and down for the word 'crooked' and stays constant for the word 'plain'. Then marvel at what a privilege it is to have access to God on the open road.

3 *December*

Chorus [3:00] – Isaiah 40:5

> *And the glory of the Lord shall be revealed, and all flesh shall see it together: for the mouth of the Lord hath spoken it.*

One of the great anticlimaxes in all of cinema is surely when Dorothy pulls back the green curtain to reveal the Wizard of Oz. The great and powerful wizard – the one who'd promised courage to the Lion, a heart to the Tin Man, brains to the Scarecrow and a return home for Dorothy – is exposed as a fraud. He is a little old man, with a very big microphone.

We've heard some wonderful promises of comfort and salvation in the early movements of *Messiah*. In today's meditation, based on Isaiah 40:5, the curtain is pulled back on who has been making them. What do we find? Has the speaker been all talk and no substance? Empty words, leading to hollow hopes? Not this time. As the smallest crack opens through the curtain, a piercing, blinding light blazes forth: the glory of the Lord shall be revealed! How fitting that the choir's first piece in *Messiah* has sopranos, altos, tenors and basses singing together of the sheer privilege all flesh will have in seeing together a disclosure of such magnificence.

Human beings are instinctive glory hunters. In the run-up to Christmas, it's so easy to be thrown off the scent for true glory – God's glory – by the allure of lesser glories. 'Here, buy this life-transforming piece of new technology!' 'Here, eat this mouthwatering festive morsel!' 'Here, enjoy this night out with friends!'

The word for glory (*kavod*) is connected to the Hebrew word for weighty or heavy (*kaved*). To have the glory of the Lord revealed is to be exposed to the sheer weightiness or heaviness, or abundance or splendour, of divine majesty. It's like opening your front door and finding the sun on your doorstep. Only it's far more than that, because the revelation of the glory of the Lord is beyond any and every comparison you could make. Here is the One who made everything from nothing, who 'hung the stars like chandeliers' and 'numbered every grain of sand'.[1] Here is the One who, from all eternity, has lived in the joyful union of Father, Son and Holy Spirit. Here is the One full of grace and truth and life and love. And here is the One who wants to reveal his very being in all its glory to you, in order to bring you spiritually home. Yes, you.

Don't settle for any old glory this Christmas. C.S. Lewis would say 'we're far too easily pleased'[2]. Isaiah would say that the very glory of the Lord will be revealed, for all the world to see! Let him capture you, enthral you, magnetise you, draw you in. Let his magnificent, magisterial gravitational pull hold your affections, fill your heart, ground your hopes.

1 Taken from the song 'God, the Uncreated One' by Keith and Kristyn Getty.

2 C.S. Lewis, 'Weight of Glory' sermon, 1941.

4 December

Bass Accompagnato [1:23] – Haggai 2:6–7; Malachi 3:1

> *Thus saith the Lord, the Lord of hosts: Yet once a little while and I will shake the heavens and the earth, the sea and the dry land. And I will shake all nations; and the desire of all nations shall come. The Lord, whom ye seek, shall suddenly come to His temple, even the messenger of the covenant, whom ye delight in: Behold, He shall come, saith the Lord of Hosts.*

It is said there are few things more terrifying than being caught in an earthquake. Solid ground shifts beneath your feet. Mighty rocks crack and split and fall. Buildings and monuments that have stood for generations crumble like castles of sand.

We've been reflecting on Isaiah's promise of the coming of the Lord. That long-hoped-for, long-awaited, long-expected day of help and salvation and deliverance. Cast your mind back to waiting for Christmas Day as an excitable eight-year-old, chalking off day after day after day. The longing and anticipation were driving you mad, which in turn was having the same effect on everyone else!

Today's meditation leaves behind the world of Isaiah and jumps ahead first to the time of Haggai (around 520 BC) and then to the time of Malachi (around 460 BC). How has the story moved on?

In Haggai, the day of deliverance has been and gone. God's people have finally returned home from exile. But instead of throwing themselves into restoring the temple and renewed lives of worship, any zeal for the Lord had been dulled by the distraction of plush home improvements. And so, the Lord upends such spiritual apathy in the strongest, cosmic terms: 'I will shake the heavens, and the earth, and the sea, and the dry land' (Haggai 2:6). In language reminiscent of his thunderous display at Mount Sinai after the Exodus, God wants no one missing out. He continues, 'And I will shake all nations, and the desire [literally, 'the treasures', ESV] of all nations shall come' (Haggai 2:7). With Israel's devotional life having fallen on hard times, the Lord arouses the whole world to join in his glorious 'worship restoration' project. With new covenant eyes, and in the modernised words of Isaac Watts, 'Let every creature rise and bring blessing and honour to their king'.[3] Will we heed Haggai's warning this Christmas? Will we give Jesus our all this festive season? Or does our devotion to God need shaking from the distraction of plush home improvements too? The Christ of Christmas must never be lost in consumerism.

That brings us to Malachi, who picks up where Haggai leaves off. God's people have come home, God's temple is finally restored. The stage has been set for God's arrival, that great culmination of so many Old Testament promises of God finally coming to live with his people. From God's side, there was never any doubt: 'Behold, he shall come, saith the LORD of hosts' (Malachi 3:1). And that box was firmly ticked in Bethlehem, at the Messiah's first advent. From our side however, as we await his second advent, the question is, are *we* ready to embrace him, both now and for eternity, as our greatest desire, above all else?

3 Taken from the hymn 'Jesus Shall Reign Where'er the Sun'.

5 December

Alto Aria [4:24] – Malachi 3:2

> *But who may abide the day of His coming, and who shall stand when He appeareth? For He is like a refiner's fire.*

Chorus [2:29] – Malachi 3:3

> *And He shall purify the sons of Levi, that they may offer unto the Lord an offering in righteousness.*

We meditated yesterday on the earth-shattering reality of the coming of the Lord. Today we are confronted with what that will mean for sinful human beings like us. The mood of the alto aria is sombre. God is a consuming fire; he will tolerate no rivals (Deuteronomy 4:24). There will be no escape for those who ignore his offer of salvation (Hebrews 12:25–29), reject his law or despise his word (Isaiah 5:24).

Yet, the very God who revealed himself in thunder and lightning on Mount Sinai declared that he is also the gracious and compassionate God, slow to anger and abounding in love. Through the atoning sacrifice of his own Son, the Lord poured out his wrath at Calvary and offers us forgiveness. 'If you, LORD, kept a record of sins … who could stand?' asks the psalmist. 'But with you there is forgiveness' (Psalm 130:3–4, NIV)!

But what of the fire for a forgiven sinner?

A few years ago, our family visited the Dartington Crystal factory in north Devon. We observed glowing furnaces of molten glass. Their purpose? To achieve a texture that can be moulded into something useful, beautiful and valuable, and to burn up impurities in the scorching 2200°F. It is an intense process for the glass, but a necessary one if you want to make world-renowned, exquisite crystal fit for a Christmas table. Handel paints the picture vividly here as agitated musical runs and leaps conjure up images of refining flames.

If we are playing fast and loose with sin, God will do what it takes to purify us. This is, in fact, astounding grace: to beautify, and not burn up, his corrupt servants. As a Kingdom of Priests, after the 'sons of Levi', God will see to it that we offer him acceptable worship. He will not stand idly by while we flirt with other gods, to our own destruction.

More often, the permitted fires of this broken creation are intended to build our character and prove to the world that God is still sovereign, good and trustworthy, even when things don't go our way (1 Peter 1:7). For the Christian, there's purpose in pain and God promises that flames will not *consume* us (Isaiah 43:2). Yes, they will make us weep; yes, they will burn up things that we were holding on to; yes, they will melt and reshape us. But they will not *ultimately* harm us. We pray that after being tested by God, you, like Job, 'will come forth as gold' (Job 23:10, NIV). May you testify with this unknown hymnwriter,

When through fiery trials thy pathway shall lie,
My grace, all sufficient, shall be thy supply;
The flame shall not hurt thee; I only design
Thy dross to consume, and thy gold to refine.[4]

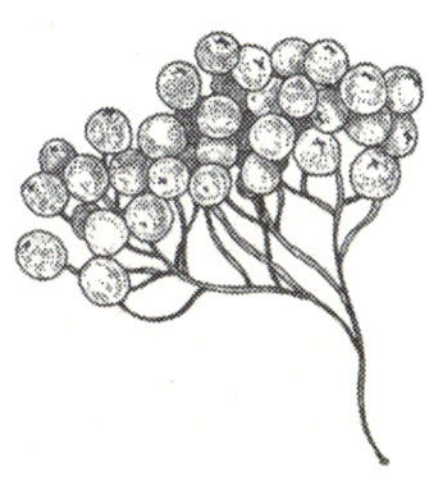

4 Taken from the hymn 'How Firm a Foundation'.

6 December

Alto Recitative [0:30] – Isaiah 7:14; Matthew 1:23

Behold, a virgin shall conceive and bear a Son, and shall call his name Emmanuel, God with us.

Alto Aria and Chorus [5:08] – Isaiah 40:9; Isaiah 60:1

O thou that tellest good tidings to Zion, get thee up into the high mountain. O thou that tellest good tidings to Jerusalem, lift up thy voice with strength; lift it up, be not afraid; say unto the cities of Judah, Behold your God! O thou that tellest good tidings to Zion, arise, shine, for thy light is come, and the glory of the Lord is risen upon thee.

Make it unmissable. That's the principle behind the launch of the latest iPhone or the release of the new Hollywood blockbuster. But God doesn't need publicity stunts. When God unveils his coming Messiah in Isaiah 7, he's been planning it since before the dawn of time, paving the way with thousands of years of flawed and insignificant characters. He slips the greatest announcement ever in an unlikely pronouncement by an unlikely prophet to an unlikely king.

This is the context: A rebellious king, Ahaz, defies God's prophet by refusing to ask for a divine sign which would back up God's promise of protection. The nation of Judah is terrified by the warmongering kings, Rezin of Syria and Pekah of Israel (Isaiah 7:1). Ahaz wants to solve Judah's international relations crisis *his* way by making a foolish alliance with the even more imposing Assyrian superpower. But God gives him a sign anyway! And it's one that apparently has nothing at all to do with Israel's military strategy and won't even be fulfilled in the king's lifetime.

What is God thinking? In Handel's *Messiah*, we hear a solo voice state out of the stillness, 'Behold, a virgin shall conceive, and bear a son.' According to God, an unnamed Son being implanted in the womb of a humble virgin, hundreds of years in the future, is the most militarily significant news Ahaz can hear right now! God is challenging Ahaz to rethink his most pressing need. What Ahaz needs isn't political diplomacy. He needs to remember *who* is with his people and trust in his promises.

And this isn't just a sign for Ahaz. It's for all 'the cities of Judah', in other words, for us all. What we need is for God to come and live with us, as Isaiah testifies: '[she] shall call his name Emmanuel, God with us'. We need the seed of a woman to come and make his dwelling among us so that ultimately God and mankind may dwell together forever in a restored creation.

Don't forget that truth this Christmas. Your most urgent need isn't to book the turkey, buy presents or get the house tidied for visitors. It is for God himself to dwell with you … in you. And that need has been met through an understated teenage pregnancy and a dirty, back-street maternity unit. 'How silently, how silently the wondrous gift is given!'

But, while the announcement of a promised Son might have *come* quietly, it's not one Isaiah wants us to stay quiet about. 'Get thee up into a high mountain'! Shout it from the rooftops. This is news which liberates people from fear ('be not afraid') and brings hope ('thy light is come'). Ask God to 'lift up thy voice with strength' this Advent. Make sure you don't keep such 'good tidings' to yourself.

7 December

Bass Accompagnato [2:35] – Isaiah 60:2–3

For behold, darkness shall cover the earth, and gross darkness the people; but the Lord shall arise upon thee, and His glory shall be seen upon thee. And the Gentiles shall come to thy light, and kings to the brightness of thy rising.

Bass Aria [3:15] – Isaiah 9:2

The people that walked in darkness have seen a great light; and they that dwell in the land of the shadow of death, upon them hath the light shined.

In 2010, thirty-three Chilean miners were trapped for sixty-nine days under 700m of rock, in a collapsed copper-gold mine in the Atacama Desert. Most of the time they had spent in complete darkness. As they were finally pulled one by one to the surface in a specially made capsule, light was synonymous with rescue. The context of our verses here in Isaiah 9:2 is an equally bleak situation. As we saw yesterday, the southern kingdom of Judah faces military threats on every side. There was, humanly speaking, no light at the end of the tunnel.

In an attempt to escape his predicament, wicked king Ahaz has sought a coalition with his enemy, paying tribute to Assyria, to secure protection! Sounds like madness, doesn't it? But are we all that different? Fumbling about in the dark, we offer homage to false gods in an attempt to find security and hope. Comfort-eating, binge-watching, people-pleasing, self-improving; we'd sooner put sticking plasters on our gaping spiritual wounds than cry out in repentance for salvation.

But God has a better solution. In his great mercy, God promises that on this land of deep darkness his light will dawn; his rescuer will come; his Son will rise. In fact, so secure is the promise, that it is made in the past tense. Notice that this is not God finally giving in to Ahaz's pleas for rescue. No, Ahaz was firmly engaged in constructing his own, temporary rescue plan. You see, God's mercy always comes first. He always takes the initiative in salvation. 'God, who is rich in mercy, made us alive with Christ even when we were dead in transgressions – it is by grace you have been saved' (Ephesians 2:4–5, NIV).

If you're a follower of Jesus today, by nature you were in deep spiritual darkness, pincered by the enemies of sin, death and the devil. No earthly coalition could help you out of that fix. You needed search and rescue. And one came that first Christmas, foretold to Ahaz and later announced to shepherds. The Light of the World descended, not 700m into the earth, but infinite depths from the highest heaven to the very pit of hell for you.

So as you light candles and drape your tree in strings of lights, don't settle for just a warm fuzzy feeling. May each light be a reminder for you of the beam of undeserved hope that has split your darkness. And it's the only hope for countless millions still walking in darkness.

8 December

Chorus [4:01] – Isaiah 9:6

> *For unto us a Child is born, unto us a Son is given, and the government shall be upon His shoulder, and His name shall be called Wonderful Counsellor, the Mighty God, the Everlasting Father, the Prince of Peace.*

Where are you up to in your Christmas shopping? While some members of the Gobbett family are usually spotted scrabbling around the shops at the eleventh hour, others have been quietly getting on with it for months. Often, the more planned ahead the shopping, the more perfect the gift. Some of our family members are complete pros.

How would you define the perfect gift? Perhaps a combination of what's most needed and what's most wanted, fitting its recipient like a glove. Often it will be for life, not just for Christmas, as the best gifts just keep on giving. And if you can add an element of surprise, so much the better.

Today we're back in Isaiah 9, with the most perfect Christmas gift, seven hundred years in the planning. The recipients are people walking out of darkness into light (Isaiah 9:2–5). Days of strife are to be replaced with days of celebration. What gift could possibly turn things around so dramatically?

The gift of a baby. A Son.

For those of us familiar with the nativity, we can now see it coming. But the idea that the birth of a baby could trigger a spiritual revolution the world over would have seemed inconceivable to its first hearers. Has there been a more surprising Christmas gift? And to hear that the authority of the world's governments rests casually on his shoulders surely beggars belief. What child is this?

He's the 'Wonderful Counsellor', the one who draws alongside us like no one else; and so, he's the perfect gift for the isolated and hurting. He's the 'Mighty God', the one with the power to overcome the greatest obstacles; and so, he's the perfect gift for the vulnerable and overwhelmed. He's the 'Everlasting Father', the one who's loved us as his own since before the dawn of time; and so, he's the perfect gift for the lonely and insecure. He's the 'Prince of Peace', the one who makes wars to cease, starting with the one between us and a holy God; and so, he's the perfect gift for the anxious and afraid.

Have you grasped how precious the gift of Jesus Christ is? Whether we know it yet or not, his gift combines what we most want with what we most need. His gift fits us like a glove. And wonder of wonders, his gift is for life and eternity, not just for Christmas. Jesus is the gift that keeps on giving, no matter how many parcels you have left to wrap.

Pifa [2:51]

Why not conclude today's reflection by listening to Handel's orchestral Pastoral Symphony and pray that God would open your eyes even wider to all that you're offered in the gift of Jesus this Christmas.

9 December

Soprano Recitative [0:19] – Luke 2:8

There were shepherds abiding in the field, keeping watch over their flocks by night.

Soprano Accompagnato [0:22] – Luke 2:9

And lo! the angel of the Lord came upon them, and the glory of the Lord shone round about them, and they were sore afraid.

Soprano Recitative [0:31] – Luke 2:10–11

And the angel said unto them, Fear not; for behold, I bring you good tidings of great joy, which shall be to all people. For unto you is born this day in the city of David a Saviour, which is Christ the Lord.

Soprano Accompagnato [0:16] – Luke 2:13

And suddenly there was with the angel a multitude of the heavenly host praising God, and saying,

Chorus [1:56] – Luke 2:14

Glory to God in the highest, and peace on earth, good will towards men.

'There were shepherds ... keeping watch over their flocks at night' (Luke 2:8, NIV). More importantly, God – the great Shepherd of his people, Israel – was keeping watch over *his* flock by night. No sooner is Mary's child born and laid in a manger than the little town of Bethlehem and its humble shepherd community is lit by a celestial nightlight. Even a glimpse of the light that surrounds the presence of God is enough to terrify the hardiest of men.

But the angels quickly dispel their fear by proclaiming good news to God's people. *All* God's people, without exception. Note that the first to be directly addressed are lowly shepherds. God has always invested in the underdog. His gospel has always been good news for the poor (Isaiah 61:1). And in God's overarching story, spiritual shepherds are the leaders of God's people. So it's only right that literal shepherds should be the ones to blaze the trail down to Bethlehem and then onwards to spread the news.

Three names are tucked away in the angels' tidings. They're easy to miss in these soprano recitatives. Who is born in the city of David? A *Saviour*, *Christ*, *the Lord*. He will bring the ultimate rescue that has eluded God's people for generations – rescue from their enemies; rescue from themselves. He is the *Christ*, the one chosen and anointed for the task, guaranteeing the effectual nature of his rescue. He is the *Lord* – not a 'get out of jail free' kind of rescuer, but a rescuer who makes demands on his people. We must revere and submit to him.

News of that kind of Saviour brings out the whole heavenly host in a chorus of praise. Does your heart sing with them? Praise God for our rescuer! He alone brings 'peace on earth'. These words carry with them sentiments of tranquillity, blessing and safety. Maybe you have fears this Advent. Fears about health, wayward loved ones, geopolitics. Rest in God's chosen, sovereign rescuer, comforted by the heavenly nightlight that illuminates his flock.

10 December

Soprano Aria [4:10] – Zechariah 9:9–10

Rejoice greatly, O daughter of Zion; shout, O daughter of Jerusalem! Behold, thy King cometh unto thee; He is the righteous Saviour, and He shall speak peace unto the heathen.

Alto Recitative [0:32] – Isaiah 35:5–6

Then shall the eyes of the blind be opened, and the ears of the deaf unstopped. Then shall the lame man leap as an hart, and the tongue of the dumb shall sing.

A week after succeeding to the throne, King Charles III visited Cardiff. Some of our friends made it to the front of the waiting crowds and managed to shake the sovereign's hand. They came back buzzing! In today's musical movement, Zechariah – a prophet to Judah on their return from exile in Babylon – offers God's people cause for great rejoicing. In the tenderest of terms, God addresses his people as 'daughter'. As they struggle to rebuild the temple in Jerusalem, they hear of something even better: Jerusalem's *King* is coming! This is the King they need for protection. In Zechariah 9, God promises to subdue (or 'speak peace unto') Judah's enemies ('the heathen'), and protect Jerusalem by his presence. He vows, 'I will encamp at my temple to guard it against marauding forces. Never again will an oppressor overrun my people, for now I am keeping watch' (Zechariah 9:8, NIV).

This is precisely what God's people have been longing to hear. It's only natural that they would 'Rejoice greatly'! We need to remember this when we bemoan the state of the nation or strive to regain some kind of 'former glory'. We live the other side of Zechariah's prophecy. The King *has* come! He already dwells with his people by his Spirit, and he's coming again to make that a physical and unchallenged reality.

King Charles was recognisable: familiar face, fine clothes, royal entourage, media presence, police escort. But when Jerusalem's king came to town, he wasn't what many people had imagined. Zechariah 9:9 tells us he would come 'lowly and riding on a donkey' (NIV). And on Palm Sunday that's exactly what he did. Those who knew their Old Testament prophecy should have recognised their King!

But the main way we can recognise God's King is by the *way* he rules. As well as subduing his kingdom's enemies, he is a *righteous Saviour*. All of his judgments are morally right and for the good of his people. Imagine that?! This is the kind of rule all the world's nations could do with. And the alto recitative which follows this aria describes more of the blessing that comes to a people ruled by such a King: blind eyes opened, deaf ears unstopped, lame leaping, mute singing. When John the Baptist was in prison and wondering if he'd picked the wrong man to follow, it was these evidences that convinced him Jesus was indeed the Messiah (Matthew 11:2–5).

Rejoice greatly for your King! Not only can he restore *physically*, but he also brings *spiritual* sight, hearing and singing. He can do that for you today, if you ask him. His healing kingdom will never end. He will reign on a renewed earth in the glorious new Jerusalem, where there will be no need to rebuild temples, for 'the Lord God Almighty and the Lamb are its temple' (Revelation 21:22, NIV).

11 December

Alto/Soprano Duet [5:38] – Isaiah 40:11; Matthew 11:28–29

He shall feed His flock like a shepherd; and He shall gather the lambs with His arm, and carry them in His bosom, and gently lead those that are with young. Come unto Him, all ye that labour, that are heavy laden, and He will give you rest. Take His yoke upon you, and learn of Him; for He is meek and lowly of heart: and ye shall find rest unto your souls.

Grazing animals cover a lot of ground! They won't be well-fed and healthy if they stay in one place, because supplies of fresh grass will be quickly depleted. That's why they must be led by a shepherd.

The Christian life follows a similar pattern. We must be constantly on the move if we're going to grow. Not geographically, necessarily, but inwardly. The writer to the Hebrews chides his readers for failing to mature spiritually, because they are not applying themselves to growth in their understanding and application of God's word (Hebrews 5:11–14).

But how does this occur? By walking faithfully and trustingly with your Good Shepherd, wherever he may lead. By listening to his voice in the Scriptures and responding in obedient faith. Like sheep, we rarely know what's good for us. But he does. He alone has the bird's-eye view and knows where the green pastures are. It may be an uphill climb; you may not be able to see around the next bend. But he knows where he's leading you, and his goal is to restore your soul (Psalm 23:3).

And how might the next meal come? In seeing for the first time a beautiful truth in the Scriptures; by being amazed afresh at an old one. In being spurred on by the encouragement or example of a new friend; by responding to the challenging voice of the timeless Spirit. In embarking on a new and exciting season of life; by leaving behind a familiar place to step out in faith. We won't grow spiritually if we remain static.

Ultimately, what we feed on is Jesus himself. After supplying food for a large flock of people on the mountainside overlooking the Sea of Galilee, Jesus told his disciples that he himself is the Living Bread (John 6:51) – bread that he gave to be broken for us. The Good Shepherd has already laid down his life for the sheep.

And do you notice *how* he leads us. He's not like the school cross-country pacesetter who strides out in front, leaving the rest of the mud-spattered class puffing and panting behind. No, he goes at a pace you can keep up with. If you're young in the faith, he'll pick you up if necessary and carry you close to his heart. If you have young in the family, he'll lead you *gently*. So lay down your fears and come follow the Shepherd. With him, you will find rest for your souls. More of this tomorrow!

12 December

Chorus [2:19] – Matthew 11:30

His yoke is easy, and His burden is light.

At the age of seventeen, I (Sally) went on a mission trip to Romania to help with children's summer camps. Back (and front!) packs were stuffed with as many resources as could be lifted. And that's not to mention the piano accordion. After a long walk across Bucharest to our accommodation, imagine the relief at laying down those burdens! But how strange it would have been if our host had then volunteered, 'Here, let me take your bags, but don't sit down because I've got a better plan to ease your aching back and blistered feet: pop this small rucksack on and we'll just go for a short walk to see some of the sights.' That would have been nonsensical!

Yet this is the mysterious paradox of the gospel. Jesus says that the way to be free of our burdens, the way to find rest, is not to cast off responsibility and put your feet up, or forge your own path and look after number one. Jesus says relief comes when we lay down *our* unbearable loads of performance, guilt, shame, self-improvement, confusion, anxiety and fear, instead yoking ourselves to him and taking *his* burden on our shoulders. The musical decoration in this movement paints a picture of the resulting freedom and lightness.

But this doesn't make sense to fallen logic, even if millions have found it to be true. It has to be tasted to be seen. How could hitching yourself to someone else, who challenges your autonomy and takes control of your direction, bring freedom? How could taking on another 'burden' possibly bring relief? It is because, we're told, his yoke is *easy*, and his burden is *light*. The word 'easy' in this verse doesn't mean 'plain-sailing' or 'a doddle'. No, Jesus promises that in this life his followers will have trouble; he calls us to take up our *cross* and follow him. Rather, the word 'easy' has the idea of not being oppressive, crushing or unbearable. His commandments are not burdensome, like those the devil, or even Pharisees, lay on people's backs.

Do you believe that being yoked to Jesus won't cramp your style, but will actually be for your good and flourishing? It will mean that he shares the load with you and will never leave your side. He will be there, by his Spirit, through it all, to listen, comfort, help, equip, encourage, challenge and guide. For, as we hear in the glorious final line of this chorus, resolving in a perfect cadence, 'his burden is light'.

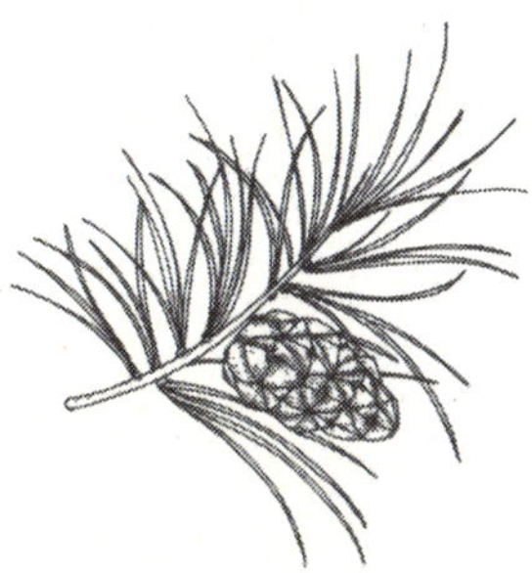

PART 2

THE *Passion* OF THE *Messiah*

13 December

Chorus [3:08] – John 1:29

Behold the Lamb of God, that taketh away the sin of the world.

One of the most sober moments in recent British history was the formation of 'The Queue' in September 2022. Nearly a quarter of a million people, from famous celebrities to members of the general public, all wanted to pay their respects to Her Late Majesty Queen Elizabeth II. And so they waited, some for over twenty-four hours, before spending a matter of seconds in silence in front of her coffin as she lay in state in Westminster Hall. They wanted to behold their servant monarch, before she was taken from view for good.

In this movement from *Messiah*, we are summoned by John the Baptist to behold an even greater servant monarch, on the way to his own funeral. This time, however, there is no pomp and ceremony; Jesus goes as a sacrificial lamb to the slaughter. Handel's music begins with a funeral march, much akin to those that accompanied the dignified procession that made its way down Long Walk, the three-mile-long avenue leading to Windsor Castle as Her Late Majesty was laid to rest in St George's Chapel. Dotted rhythms here denote royalty, while the descending melody line communicates impending doom. This lamb is not the cute and cuddly variety of a school nativity. He is a bloodstained offering, slain on the temple altar to atone for the death-deserving sin of God's people – though he himself was sinless, without blemish or spot, as required by the Levitical law (Leviticus 22:20; 1 Peter 1:19).

At the time John makes his declaration, Jesus hasn't even begun his formal ministry. He hasn't even been baptised by John yet or experienced the wilderness temptations. But John, by the inspiration of the Holy Spirit, knows just where Jesus is headed. Jesus too knew just where he was headed, and the prophecies also foretold that the suffering servant would be led like a lamb to the slaughter (Isaiah 53:7).

So take a pause now in the busyness of Advent to behold this Lamb. Behold his innocence and purity; behold his submission; behold his dignity; behold his self-giving love. And behold the seriousness of your sin which demands such atonement. Resolve again to take *it* to the slaughter and worship only the Lamb of God.

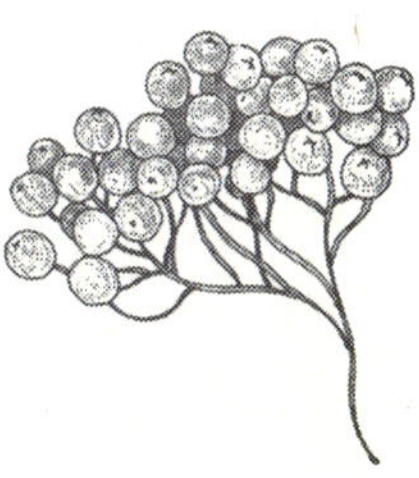

14 December

Alto Aria [11:34] – Isaiah 53:3; 50:6

> *He was despised and rejected of men, a man of sorrows and acquainted with grief. He gave His back to the smiters, and His cheeks to them that plucked off the hair: He hid not His face from shame and spitting.*

This haunting aria is by far the longest movement in the whole of *Messiah*, positioned at its exact midpoint. The despicable reality unfolded before us is right at the heart of the Christian gospel. We must not rush away from it. Handel will not let us move on until the full horror of the scene has been felt. It must change us forever.

Miscarriages of justice appal us. Few things stir our spirits to cry out like seeing the innocent unfairly punished. The tragic mistreatment of countless upstanding Post Office workers as a result of the Horizon IT scandal between 1999 and 2015 is a painful example. The strength of an outcry must correspond to the degree of innocence and brutality involved.

Pay attention to the opening section of this aria. As each mournful phrase is sighed out, punctuated by a gaping violin interlude, ask yourself, 'Who is *he* that was treated thus?' Let each heinous injustice sink in. The one despised and rejected here was none other than the aforementioned Lamb of God, the spotless One, the One without blemish or defect. Handel has already revealed this Lamb as the same Glorious One of Isaiah 40; the Consuming Fire of Malachi 3; Immanuel; Wonderful

Counsellor; Mighty God; Everlasting Father; Prince of Peace; Jerusalem's coming King; the righteous Saviour; the One who gives sight to the blind; the meek and lowly Shepherd; the One who gives rest. Here is the ultimate miscarriage of justice.

Yet see how silently this Lamb goes to the slaughter. The One who loosened the tongue of the mute does not open his mouth. As the music transitions to a relentless, pulsating, central section, waves of anguish give way to a swirling storm of merciless abuse. An agitated voice spits out 'back', 'smiters', 'cheeks', 'plucked', 'spitting'. Are these not the strong bulls, roaring lions and villainous dogs that surround the foretold Messiah of Psalm 22?

But the marvel of the gospel is this: Jesus was not cornered in these scenes. No, he *chose* this path; he submitted to the Father, though even the contemplation of it caused the blood vessels in his skin to rupture in Gethsemane. Isaiah 50:6 reminds us Jesus *offered* his back and his cheeks to those who struck him. When they hurled their insults at him, he did not retaliate. Men hid their faces from him, such was their loathing; but he did not hide his face from shame.

As the opening lament resumes to close this movement, linger here a moment. How will you respond? Apparently when a friend entered Handel's room as he was composing it, he found Handel sobbing. 'Godly sorrow brings repentance that leads to salvation and leaves no regret' (2 Corinthians 7:10, NIV).

15 December

Chorus [2:00] – Isaiah 53:4–5

> *Surely He hath borne our griefs, and carried our sorrows! He was wounded for our transgressions, He was bruised for our iniquities; the chastisement of our peace was upon Him.*

Chorus [1:53] – Isaiah 53:5

> *And with His stripes we are healed.*

Today we move from the facts of Christ's passion to its reason. *Why* did Jesus die? From a purely historic perspective, it was because hateful men crucified him. An unholy alliance between the Roman authorities and the religious leaders 'despised and rejected him' (Isaiah 53:3), as we saw yesterday, leading to his crucifixion.

But the Bible gives further perspectives. Though written seven hundred years before the event, Isaiah's prophecy makes it abundantly clear that Jesus suffered and died *because of us*. Did you note that repeated word in verses 4 and 5? Our. It occurs five times in two verses. *Our* griefs; *our* sorrows; *our* transgressions; *our* iniquities; the chastisement of *our* peace was upon him.

Jesus didn't *need* to die. But he chose to die.

Cast your mind back to Sally's travel rucksack on Day 12. Now replace holiday items and mission resources with scores and scores of notebooks. Imagine every time you've ever stepped over the line, throughout your life, it's all been written in a notebook and placed inside the rucksack. Every exaggeration, every lustful thought, every outburst of anger, every act of greed, every self-righteous criticism: it's all logged and stuffed in the bag. And all sin's ghastly effects are included too. The shame. The guilt. The regret. The hurt. The damaged relationships. The broken dreams. With notebook after notebook, catalogue after sorry catalogue, how long before the rucksack's seams start to burst? How long before you can barely lift it off the ground? But carry it you must, all day, every day. It's a back-breaking and crushing load. And yet Jesus willingly took it all, and for all who look to him as their only hope. 'He took my sins and my sorrows and made them his very own, he bore the burden to Calvary and suffered and died alone.'

People sometimes talk wistfully about 'carrying their regrets to the grave'. But Jesus has done that for us already. 'Leave them with me,' he's saying; 'I'll take them from here.' Little wonder so many find such comfort in hearing the words of Handel's *Messiah* sung to them each Christmas. After one such early performance in London, Lord Kinnoull wrote personally to Handel to congratulate him for bringing such 'noble entertainment' to the city. Handel is said to have replied, 'My Lord, I should be sorry if I only entertained them; I wished to make them better.'

'With his stripes we are healed.'

16 December

Chorus [4:12] – Isaiah 53:6

All we like sheep have gone astray; we have turned every one to his own way. And the Lord hath laid on Him the iniquity of us all.

The music that accompanies today's movement takes many by surprise. We are carrying on our meditation on the suffering of Jesus Christ, as foretold by the prophet Isaiah. We've been haunted by the alto's harrowing Aria ('He Was Despised', Day 14). We've been arrested by the heartfelt crescendo of the Chorus ('Surely He Hath Borne Our Griefs', Day 15). We have reached the very heart of the Christian gospel: the divine purpose of the cross of Christ. Truly we're standing on holy ground.

Then suddenly Handel's arrangement of 'All We Like Sheep' bursts into life, with all the energy and excitement of children early on Christmas morning. What's with the mood change? Do not the circumstances surrounding Jesus' death require something more *sober*?

Then again, we're talking about sheep. And sheep are wayward. They wander. And they frolic and jump and run and hide and tumble all over each over. Handel captures it all brilliantly. Phrase echoes phrase, and confession follows confession, as the various singers call to one another of our universal plight. Each line of melody recreates the biblical text: our waywardness ('have gone astra-a-a-a-a-a-ay'); our wanderings ('we have tu-u-u-u-urned'); and our unique, distinctly individual ways of doing so (the staccato 'ev-ry-one to his own way').

The American cartoonist Gary Larson illustrates Isaiah 53:6 with a picture of a sheep, wearing a dog collar and standing behind a pulpit. His text is: 'All we like humans have gone astray'. To be a sheep is to go astray. To be a human is sadly to do the same.

But Handel's lyrics continue. Suddenly the light and frolicking melody descends into the heaviest, most sombre tones: 'And the Lord … hath … laid … on … Him … the ini-qui-ty of us all.' We've arrived at the epicentre of the Christian faith. We asked yesterday: Why did Jesus die? Not just because of hateful men. Not just because of our sin. Ultimately, Jesus died because it 'was the LORD's will to crush him' (Isaiah 53:10, NIV). Jesus willingly endured God's rightful anger at our sin, in our place.

Captain Corelli's Mandolin tells the story of occupied Cephalonia. Captain Antoni Corelli faces the firing squad for being on the wrong side. His loyal friend Carlo Guercio stands at his side. As soon as the order to fire has been given, and while no one is looking, Carlo quietly steps sideways in front of Corelli. Corelli tries to move away, but can't. Carlo is grasping hold of his fists and not letting him go. And then the bullets start to fly. One bullet after another burrow themselves into Carlo's enormous frame, 'like white-hot parasitic knives into the muscle of his chest. He … flung himself over backwards. Corelli lay beneath him, paralysed by his weight, drenched utterly in his blood, stupefied by an act of love.'[5]

For those of us wayward sheep who've sheltered in Christ for salvation, we are all Antoni Corelli.

5 Louis de Bernieres, *Captain Corelli's Mandolin* (Vintage, 1998), p. 325.

17 December

Tenor Accompagnato [0:51] – Psalm 22:7

All they that see Him laugh Him to scorn; they shoot out their lips, and shake their heads, saying:

Chorus [2:21] – Psalm 22:8

He trusted in God that He would deliver Him: let Him deliver Him, if He delight in Him.

Tenor Accompagnato [2:06] – Psalm 69:20

Thy rebuke hath broken His heart: He is full of heaviness. He looked for some to have pity on Him, but there was no man, neither found He any to comfort Him.

Tenor Arioso [1:33] – Lamentations 1:12

Behold, and see if there be any sorrow like unto His sorrow.

Tenor or Soprano Accompagnato [0:18] – Isaiah 53:8

He was cut off out of the land of the living: for the transgressions of thy people was He stricken.

What did the cross *feel like* for Jesus? Perhaps it sounds like a strange question to ask, but it's important to do so. As we consider the divine purpose in Christ's suffering, we have to be careful not to assume that Jesus had some kind of spiritual 'override' button that lessened his personal anguish. We must never suppose he had a mysterious, God-given capacity to cope with far more than us mere mortals.

Today we focus on the human side of Jesus' suffering. 'The Emotional Life of Our Lord' was an important essay by nineteenth-century theologian B.B. Warfield. He argued that because Jesus is God incarnate, he was able to experience the fullest range of emotions that anyone has ever known – the greatest joys that reach the heights, and the greatest sorrows that plumb the depths; all in the right proportion, and yet all without sin.

The scene is set with the Lord Jesus strung up like a common criminal. Bearing a crown of thorns, with pierced hands and feet, a spear has just lanced his side. The fiery noonday heat ravages his body. The suffocating weight of human sin and divine judgment crush his soul. Silently he sobs. His torment is compounded by the gleeful cries of his mockers, who 'laugh Him to scorn'. 'He trusted in God', they say, 'that He would deliver Him: let Him deliver Him, if He delight in Him' (Psalm 22:7–8).

How does Jesus feel? Like no other human has ever felt before or since. Hanging naked and alone, God's 'rebuke hath broken His heart' (Psalm 69:20). Indeed, the saddest book in the Bible, Lamentations, invites us to 'behold, and see if there be any sorrow like unto His sorrow' (1:12).

This means that whatever trials or griefs are threatening to overwhelm us this Christmas, even if no one else understands, Jesus does. He gets us more than we can possibly know. And he loves to help. 'Our tendency is to feel intuitively that the more difficult life gets, the more alone we are ... The Bible corrects us. Our pain never outstrips what he himself shares in. We are never alone.'[6]

---

6 Dane Ortlund, *Gentle and Lowly* (Crossway, 2020), p. 157.

18 December

Tenor or Soprano Aria [2:22] – Psalm 16:10

But Thou didst not leave His soul in hell, nor didst Thou suffer Thy Holy One to see corruption.

Chorus [2:22] – Psalm 24:7–10

Lift up your heads, O ye gates; and be ye lift up, ye everlasting doors; and the King of Glory shall come in. Who is this King of Glory? The Lord strong and mighty, the Lord mighty in battle. Lift up your heads, O ye gates; and be ye lift up, ye everlasting doors; and the King of Glory shall come in. Who is this King of Glory? The Lord of Hosts, He is the King of Glory.

If you grew up in church and can't remember a time when you didn't know the gospel story, then first, praise God for his kindness and grace in your life; but second, recognise that sometimes the sheer wonder of the Lord Jesus' resurrection can easily be lost on you. Our family once had a glimpse of what it looks like to not know how the story ends. We'd been reading together C.S. Lewis' *The Lion, the Witch and the Wardrobe* and reached the part where Aslan dies. Tears were in full flow as our children heard of his brutal execution at the Stone Table. We let the moment hang for what (to them) seemed like an eternity, before continuing to read:

They looked around. There, shining in the sunrise, larger than they had seen him before, shaking his mane (for it had apparently grown again) stood Aslan himself.

At this point jaws hit the floor and eyes popped out of heads.

'Aren't you dead then, dear Aslan?' said Lucy.

'Not now,' said Aslan ... 'When a willing victim who had committed no treachery was killed in a traitor's stead, the Table would crack and Death itself would start working backwards.'[7]

The family burst into celebration. Aslan lives! In an instant everything changed. It was as if a light had been turned on, never to go off again. Just recalling the memory has me beaming. Aslan lives! And if you think *that* brings joy to the heart, remember afresh, dear Christian, the wonder of the truth that the tomb is gloriously empty. After nine consecutive movements plumbing the depths of Calvary, we at long last come up for breath. For God 'didst not leave His soul in hell, nor didst Thou suffer Thy Holy One to see corruption.' Jesus really lives! This indeed changes everything.

How will you respond to our risen King? Psalm 24:7–10 pictures a triumphal entry. Originally written to welcome the ark of God into Jerusalem, with gospel eyes we see heaven's gates standing to attention to receive our victorious and exalted Messiah. 'Once the babe of Bethlehem, now the Lord of History.'[8] He is the King of Glory! And to know him as Saviour and friend, is to join a revolution where death itself works backwards.

---

7 C.S. Lewis, *The Lion, the Witch and the Wardrobe* (HarperCollins Publishers, 2001), p. 174–76.

8 Taken from the song 'Joy Has Dawned upon the Earth' by Keith and Kristyn Getty.

19 December

Alto Aria [3:08] – Psalm 68:18

Thou art gone up on high. Thou hast led captivity captive, and received gifts for men, yea, even from Thine enemies, that the Lord God might dwell among them.

Chorus [1:12] – Psalm 68:11

The Lord gave the word: great was the company of the preachers.

Soprano Aria [2:08] – Romans 10:15; Isaiah 52:7

How beautiful are the feet of them that preach the gospel of peace, and bring glad tidings of good things.

Chorus [1:44] – Romans 10:18; Psalm 19:4

Their sound is gone out into all lands, and their words unto the ends of the world.

If you're on the winning side, you want the world to know. That's why every Boxing Day walk will see children proudly wearing their new Liverpool/Manchester City/____________________[9] football kits for the world to see. We're not surprised when we see them, because there's no shame in publicly identifying with

9 Delete or include as applicable. I couldn't bring myself to include West Ham, though they did win the Europa Conference League in 2023.

your victorious heroes. Who wouldn't want to join the PR team of the champions?

Today's meditation begins with the ascension of our victorious Messiah. Having won our salvation by dying on the cross and rising from the grave, Jesus has 'gone up on high' (Psalm 68:18). This phrase refers to his glorious return to the Father in heaven, with all the fanfare that we saw yesterday from Psalm 24. But with the risen and ascended Jesus now out of the picture here on earth, how does the message of our champion continue to spread?

Answer: through you and me. Well strictly speaking, first in line are 'the company of the preachers' (Psalm 68:11), who are responsible for bringing 'glad tidings of good things' (Romans 10:15). However, in Ephesians 4:8–12, the apostle Paul applies Psalm 68 by explaining that the risen Christ gave the preachers and other full-time gospel workers to equip *all* God's people to serve him. This means, in a secondary sense, that anyone who's trusted in Christ as their Saviour and Lord is recruited to be part of his PR team. God wants the gospel's 'sound [to go] out into all lands, and their words unto the ends of the world.' The news is too wonderful to keep to ourselves.

You may feel like you have very little to contribute to God's mission. Perhaps you don't have the gift of the gab. You don't have many unbelieving friends. You've got issues of your own still to work through. But as the holiday season approaches, have a go at inviting that colleague to a carol service, or hosting a drinks party for your neighbours, or including a word of testimony in a Christmas card. Then regardless of which football team's kit you might or might not be tempted to don, underneath the sports socks you'll find beautiful feet.

20 December

Bass Aria [2:46] – Psalm 2:1–2

Why do the nations so furiously rage together, and why do the people imagine a vain thing? The kings of the earth rise up, and the rulers take counsel together against the Lord, and against His anointed.

Chorus [1:53] – Psalm 2:3

Let us break their bonds asunder, and cast away their yokes from us.

Tenor Recitative [0:15] – Psalm 2:4

He that dwelleth in heaven shall laugh them to scorn; the Lord shall have them in derision.

Tenor Aria [2:15] – Psalm 2:9

Thou shalt break them with a rod of iron; thou shalt dash them in pieces like a potter's vessel.

After a beautiful aria commending beautiful feet which bring a beautiful gospel of peace, the ensuing scene could not be uglier. The rulers of the nations plot a coup against the 'King of Glory'. They are irate that anyone should threaten their supremacy.

The psalmist describes their comeback as 'a vain thing' – a futile attempt to usurp the omnipotent Lord. God has installed his king on Zion. It's a done deal. And so, God 'shall laugh them to scorn'; he 'shall have them in derision'. He laughs that one with the relative size and power of a grasshopper (Isaiah 40:22) should try to stand in his way. He laughed when Caesar Augustus called a census to establish control and taxation in his empire but unwittingly moved the unborn King of Glory to the prophesied place of his birth. He laughed at little King Herod's vain attempt to wipe out the Lord's anointed from Bethlehem and preserve his own fleeting rule as King of the Jews. That attempt only fulfilled the prophecy, 'Out of Egypt I called my son' (Matthew 2:15, NIV).

But the comeback of these earthly kings is also *tragic*. There is only one way this contest will end. They will be rebuked in God's anger, broken with a rod of iron, dashed to pieces like a potter's vessel. Their demise is profoundly sad too, since the one on whom God's government rests is called Wonderful (Isaiah 9:6). The yoke they are throwing off would have been easy and light, but this is the self-destructive character of sin. The fallen nature craves autonomy at all costs, even when the attempt is futile and leads to certain ruin. With Satan of John Milton's epic poem, 'Paradise Lost', they declare, 'Better to reign in hell than serve in heav'n'.

Perhaps you are weighed down by the way world leaders apparently flaunt God's rule, shaking off his moral code, persecuting his church. Christmas TV programmes mock, political speeches patronise. Dictators and militants outright defy. Yes, it is right to lament, deeply. But hold on with hope as well. For, make no mistake; they will not ultimately triumph.

Perhaps there are areas of your life where you yourself are dabbling in insurrection, squirming out from Christ's yoke. The final verses of Psalm 2 warn all people, to 'serve the LORD with fear', for 'blessed are all who take refuge in him' (verses 11–12, NIV).

21 December

Chorus [3:57] – Revelation 19:6; 11:15; 19:16

> *Hallelujah! for the Lord God Omnipotent reigneth. The Kingdom of this world is become the Kingdom of our Lord, and of His Christ: and He shall reign for ever and ever. King of kings, and Lord of lords.*

If you've ever seen Handel's *Messiah* performed live, you'll know that it's customary for the congregation to stand during the Hallelujah Chorus. Rumour has it that King George II was so moved by the oratorio at its London premiere in 1743 that he stood in awe of what he was hearing until the movement had finished. And if the king stands to attention, then so does everyone else. Sadly, there's no actual evidence for the rumour (or even that George II ever heard *Messiah*) and so it seems to be one of those apocryphal stories that we should file under 'wish it were true'. We can be more confident however with Handel's own recorded response to the Hallelujah Chorus. As he put the finishing touches to it, he turned to his servant with tears in his eyes and said, 'I thought I could see all heaven opened before me, and the great God himself upon his throne.'

The Hallelujah Chorus is the best-known movement in *Messiah*, perhaps even in all of Handel's works. 'Flash mobs' perform it in shopping centres. It appears regularly on classical Christmas albums. And speaking personally, I (Dave) have yet to hear it sung live without a shiver up my spine and a tear in my eye. Such is the power of fusing world-shaping theology with world-class music.

The word Hallelujah comes straight from the Hebrew, meaning 'praise ye' (*hal(e)lu-*) 'the Lord' (*-jah*). The Hallelujah Chorus transports us into heaven, peeling back the veil on spiritual realities as they are now and as they soon shall be. While politicians and presidents jostle for global significance, above them all, 'the Lord God Omnipotent reigneth ... and He shall reign for ever and ever.' Our God holds the destiny of the world in the palm of his hands. His nail-scarred hands. What confidence this gives!

Right now, it can often feel that evil and instability are in the driving seat. But one day, when the Lord Jesus returns to judge the world, every knee will bow before him. And on that day, the former Dutch Prime Minister Abraham Kuyper's famous words will be shown to be fully and finally and forever true: 'There is no square inch over which Christ, who is sovereign, does not say, "mine."'

Many people assume the Hallelujah Chorus would be the grand finale to Handel's *Messiah*. A congregation standing to attention, a rousing showstopper, ending with rapturous applause. But several more movements follow. Why is this? I wonder if it's because the fact that Jesus Christ is King of kings and Lord of lords has further implications. What does it mean to be the people of the Messiah? It's to this question we turn in our final Christmas meditations, starting tomorrow.

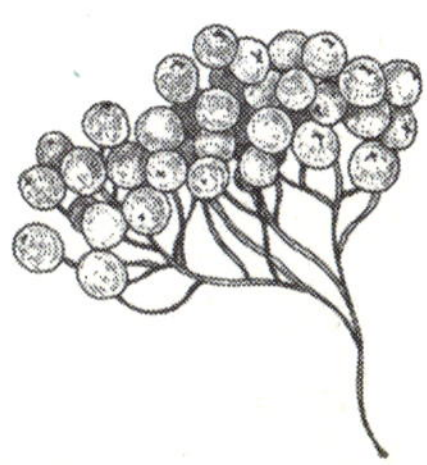

PART 3

THE *People* OF THE *Messiah*

22 *December*

Soprano Aria [6:20] – Job 19:25–26; 1 Corinthians 15:20

I know that my Redeemer liveth, and that He shall stand at the latter day upon the earth. And though worms destroy this body, yet in my flesh shall I see God. For now is Christ risen from the dead, the first fruits of them that sleep.

There is the world of difference between Christian doctrine and Christian testimony. Both are vital. Christian doctrine states truths about God and his world objectively. Christ has died, Christ has risen, Christ will come again: all statements which are gloriously true, hallelujah (see Day 21)! But the Bible insists that demons believe Christian doctrine, and tremble (James 2:19). Christian testimony takes truths about God and his world to heart, personally. It owns them subjectively. Christ has died *for me*, Christ has risen *for me*, Christ will come again *for me*.

We're up to Day 22 of our journey through Advent with Handel's *Messiah* and we've arrived at our first and only first-person singular pronouns placed on the lips of a believer: 'I know that my Redeemer liveth' (Job 19:25–26). These words were spoken initially by Job, a man who had literally lost everything. He had every reason to lose hope. But Christian doctrine led to Christian testimony. Let's slow down and marvel at the privilege of stating and owning his words for ourselves.

- 'I know': This is no second-hand knowledge ('my parents know'; 'my spouse knows'; 'my friend knows'; 'the theology books tell me'), but rather a personal confession of the deepest conviction.

- '... that my Redeemer': Redemption language comes from the slave market, but Jesus didn't purchase just anyone by paying the price for sins. He purchased *me*. He has set *me* free, forever.
- '... liveth': And having died my death, my Redeemer lives! Death, that savage master and destroyer of dreams, did not have the last word for Jesus.
- '... and that He shall stand at the latter day upon the earth': My risen Saviour will one day return! In person. Embodied. To renew and restore creation.
- '... And though worms destroy this body, yet in my flesh shall I see God': And I will see him! In person. With my own eyes. Yes, I will have to pass through death's dark veil too. Yes, the worms will first get to work on me. But when Jesus returns, I will be made new. Never to die again.

Will Job's words be your words this Christmas? Is Christian doctrine also Christian testimony for you?

Corrie ten Boom experienced much suffering. A reflection attributed to her puts this well: 'You may never know that Jesus is all you need, until Jesus is all you have.' This means that if you have lost a precious relationship this year, but you know Jesus, you're the most loved person in the world. If you fail your exams next year, but you know Jesus, you will graduate top of the class, spiritually. If you're dreading the hospital appointment in the new year, but you know Jesus, you're forever safe in his arms.

23 December

Chorus [2:31] – 1 Corinthians 15:21–22

Since by man came death, by man came also the resurrection of the dead. For as in Adam all die, even so in Christ shall all be made alive.

Bass Accompagnato [0:40] – 1 Corinthians 15:51–52

Behold, I tell you a mystery; we shall not all sleep, but we shall all be changed, in a moment, in the twinkling of an eye, at the last trumpet.

Bass Aria [8:33] – 1 Corinthians 15:52–53

The trumpet shall sound, and the dead shall be raised incorruptible, and we shall be changed. For this corruptible must put on incorruption, and this mortal must put on immortality.

Last Advent, the family photo we chose for our Christmas card needed a little airbrushing. I don't mean the grey hairs and wrinkles – tempting as that was! I mean that the contrast needed to be intensified. In this movement, Handel turns up the contrast to 100. The eerily quiet, minor-key, renaissance-style, 'Since by man came death' contrasts in every way with the ensuing outburst of 'by man came also the resurrection of the dead', complete with full orchestra and organ accompaniment.

The contrast is stark – death and life. Two polar-opposite states of humanity, brought in by two representative men: Adam and

Christ. Everyone 'in Adam' (the whole of humanity) will die. Everyone 'in Christ' (a subset of humanity) will be made alive.

In the beginning, God appointed the representative man, Adam, to commence the rule of God's image-bearers over his creation. But Adam chose to conduct affairs according to his own desires. And with humanity's rebellion came spiritual and physical death. From bitterness to bombs and temper tantrums to terrorism, mankind's total depravity reverberates through homes and nations. Wrinkles to rheumatism and colds to cancer, the ravages of disease and death surround us.

But, as dire as the human condition *in Adam* is, the second representative man, Christ, brings hope. 'Our shame was deeper than the sea; [his] grace is deeper still'.[10] After pronouncing our fallen natural condition, Paul declares in 1 Corinthians 15:22 that every man, woman and child 'in Christ' *will* be made alive.

Last summer, we took a canoe down the River Wye. There was not a breath of wind. At intervals, we stopped paddling to experience the rare jewel that is near-silence. But in those moments, our course was set by the prior direction of the canoe we were in. Where *it* went, *we* went. Those who are united to Christ will go where he has gone. And Christ has been gloriously, bodily resurrected. At the last trumpet, when Christ comes in glory, all those who have been united to him by faith will instantaneously receive full and final physical renewal. A day is coming when the shackles of sin will fall off forever. The exhaustion, pain and heartbreak of this cursed creation will end. And God's people will be eternally, magnificently alive.

10 Taken from the song 'You Alone Can Rescue' by Matt Redman.

24 *December*

Soprano Aria [4:39] – Romans 8:31, 33–34

If God be for us, who can be against us? Who shall lay anything to the charge of God's elect? It is God that justifieth. Who is he that condemneth? It is Christ that died, yea rather, that is risen again, who is at the right hand of God, and also makes intercession for us.

I wonder how you're feeling as you look back over the past year. Proud of your achievements? Loved by all? Conscience clear? More likely, you carry regrets, disappointments, insecurities and shame. Our dependence on the approval of others is a ball and chain in the Christian life, sapping our joy. Before Handel closes his masterpiece in final praise to the victorious Lamb, he wants us to grasp with both hands the full effect of the foretelling, incarnation, passion and resurrection of the Messiah. Before we embark on a new year, God wants this to shape how we look back and go forward.

Romans chapter 8 is book-ended with this astounding truth: there is no condemnation for anyone who has been joined by faith to Christ. Our status before God has changed. The righteousness we have failed to achieve by obeying the law, Christ has achieved *for* us by perfectly obeying God's law and then making himself an offering for sin (Romans 8:3–4). This is the culmination of everything we have heard to this point. One day the 'glory of the Lord will be revealed' (Isaiah 40:5, NIV, Day 3), and 'who can stand when he appears?' (Malachi 3:2, NIV, Day 5). Answer: those who are justified by faith in Christ will stand, because 'the chastisement of our peace was upon him' (Isaiah 53:5, Day 15).

'It is God that justifieth!' God has wiped the slate clean. So, neither the devil nor anyone else has the right to condemn you. To do so would be to negate the cross of Christ. In the cosmic courtroom, we have been declared 'not guilty'.

It is so hard for us to get our heads round our justification that Handel repeats the rhetorical question multiple times: 'Who can be against us?' The implied answer is 'No one!' 'Who shall lay anything to the charge of God's elect?' 'No one!' 'Who is he that condemneth?' 'No one!' If God says we are righteous, then it's irrelevant what anyone else says.

So, as you look back, view the last twelve months through gospel lenses. And go forwards into the new year in the power of the Spirit. Celebrate the freedom and life he brings. In the words of Romans 8, set your mind on what the Spirit desires (verse 5); put to death the misdeeds of the body (verse 13); live as a child of God (verse 16); and eagerly await the redemption of your sinful body (verse 23), knowing that Christ is forever at the right hand of God, making intercession for you.

25 December

Chorus [3:31] – Revelation 5:12–13

Worthy is the Lamb that was slain, and hath redeemed us to God by His blood, to receive power, and riches, and wisdom, and strength, and honour, and glory, and blessing. Blessing and honour, glory and power be unto Him that sitteth upon the throne and unto the Lamb, for ever and ever.

Chorus [3:47]

Amen.

Have you ever wanted a moment to last forever? Perhaps it was a special holiday, a breathtaking view, or a Christmas concert, like Handel's *Messiah*! Whenever we get a glimpse of glory, of exquisite beauty, or near-perfect happiness, even our weary, finite hearts want the experience to never end.

Handel's triumphant finale to *Messiah* lifts our eyes to heaven's throne room. We see a Lamb standing in the middle of the throne, looking as if it has been slain. An angel searches for someone worthy to open a scroll, sealed by seven seals, symbolic of God's cosmic plans. A weeping apostle John almost gives up hope of finding someone qualified to open the scroll. And then, up steps the Lamb.

At this, heaven's courts erupt in a song of endless praise. They sing of why the Lamb is worthy to open the scroll – because he was slain, and with his blood he purchased persons from every people group on earth. By laying down his life, as an atoning sacrifice, Jesus opened the way into the Holy of Holies, for all nations. For this slain Lamb of God is also the sovereign Lion of Judah, the Root of David, the one from Israel's royal line whose reign and kingdom was always going to be universal and eternal.

So Handel employs another fugue in his honour. This time, the overlapping voices echo the ceaseless chorus that rises from a multicultural multitude: 'Blessing and honour, glory and power be unto Him that sitteth upon the throne [God the Father] and unto the Lamb [God the Son].' Layer upon layer of praise is poured on the one who so masterfully and mercifully redeemed wretched sinners at the infinite cost of his own blood.

Praise is an experience that is simultaneously God-exalting and soul-satisfying. As C.S. Lewis insightfully put it, 'we delight to praise what we enjoy because the praise not merely expresses but completes the enjoyment.'[11] Or, in the words of the Heidelberg Catechism, 'The chief end of man is to glorify God and enjoy him forever.'

The words 'for ever and ever' are repeated sixteen times before the final 'Amen's total nearly fifty. But that doesn't even scratch the surface. Handel's glorious oratorio sadly has to come to an end. You have to eventually open the last door of the Advent calendar and put the remains in recycling. But not so with God's praise. In the words of Joseph Addison's heartwarming hymn, 'Through all eternity to thee, a joyful song I'll raise; for O, eternity's too short to utter all thy praise.'[12]

We were once involved in a 'Come-and-Sing' *Messiah* in which members of the public could turn up and join the chorus. As we close our studies this Advent, we invite you to 'come and sing' with the heavenly chorus, 'Worthy is the Lamb'. Redeemed loved ones who have gone before us are already singing. Hallelujah!

---

11 C.S. Lewis, 'Weight of Glory' sermon,1941.

12 Taken from the hymn 'When All Thy Mercies, O My God'.